Dancing in B

For the one who prophesied –
'We'll meet on the dance floor.'

Elaine Baker

V.

Published in the United Kingdom in 2023
by V. Press,
10 Vernon Grove,
Droitwich,
Worcestershire,
WR9 9LQ.

ISBN: 978-1-7394122-0-3

Cover photo & design © Sarah Leavesley, 2023
Printed in the U. K. on FSC accredited paper by 4edge Limited, www.4edge.co.uk/

Acknowledgements

For Matthew

With thanks and praise to Abba, Father

*The writing of this book was influenced by the track 'Marea (We've lost dancing)' by
Fred Again, with lyrics sampled from the Blessed Madonna (Atlantic Records, 2021)
and also by the book, Dancing in Odessa by Ilya Kaminsky (Arc Publications, 2014).*

*'The secret history of anger (1 & 2)' is a phrase from 'In praise of laughter' in Dancing
in Odessa and is a response to that poem.*

*'Prayer' uses the phrase 'If I speak for the dead' from 'Author's Prayer' in Dancing in
Odessa and is a response to that poem.*

*'Water' features the song 'Heaven is a place on earth' by Belinda Carlilse, lyrics by Rick
Nowels & Ellen Shipley, from the album Heaven on earth (MCA Records, 1987).*

*'A busker plays Amy' features lyrics from the song 'Love is a losing game' by Amy
Winehouse, from the album Back to Black (Universal Island Records, 2006). The poem
was first published in Poetry Society's Poetry News, Winter 2022.*

*'Swing low, sweet chariot' takes its title from an African-American spiritual with the
same title, composed by Wallace Willis, date unknown.*

*'Kings' features lyrics from the hymn 'We Three Kings Of Orient Are' by John Henry
Hopkins Junior, 1857.*

Contents

Prologue

The secret history of anger (1)

After 'In Praise of Laughter' by Ilya Kaminsky

In the secret history of anger, one woman keeps silence. She keeps silence all night, watching for the dawn.

In the stillest hours, the city cries and hides itself.

The woman keeps silence, watching for the dawn. God sees her thoughts, lets them fall. Petals rain on wet sands.

The city pleads for mercy.

The woman keeps silence.

She keeps silence all night.

This pan-world

Faces of clocks shut themselves.
Across the city, a bell sounds
like loneliness
or, perhaps,
a call to prayer.
We kneel; faces fall into softness,
ancient soil, strata
of good and evil.
Did we do wrong?
It's hard to breathe
with your mouth full.

Rain falls
across the face of the whole earth
for the first time
since time began.
The city is washed,
rattled in its own pan,
shaken over and over again.
Where is the gold?
Outside the city walls,
we dig holes,
to collect what falls.

Act One

Bridge

One city to another. It's been too long. You smile at me, from a well-kept lawn on Instagram. I stand on a bridge, background of cubic apartments and chunks of sky, smile back. We both know it's not simple, not simple at all; there are cracks like forked lightning breaking out across the dry lawn, up the concrete. There are sunspots in our eyes.

Today, the update says: *zero*. No number of deaths. Total eclipse. A circle of people saying nothing, and not holding hands.

The *oh* has grown like a sink hole between us and into this nothing, we've poured many things – we don't deny it. I'm too tired to text. I forget

your beautiful face.

Sirens

On the scrubby verges of the ring road, seagulls litter pick. Grainy
clouds gather overhead, cut out light. People in houses bang their
windows shut. More gulls swipe down, agitate, expel sound. They
know the scent of advancing rain but they don't know what
███████████ smells like.

City Library

Its concrete walls absorb the sun, dwell on it. Deep inside the hive, in between the shelves, the rows and rows, the spines sleep. A heavy door sighs shut. News from the outside is as irrelevant as thunder over foreign mountains.

The desks are peopled with statues, like bronzes. The only way we know they live is by their infrequent blinks, the barely perceptible rising and falling of their fabric faces

in

out.

Beyond the windows, in Chapel Gardens, an old man drives a mower over grass: one way; then back the other.

Here; now gone.

Open a window, catch a seed.

Water

Hottest day. There are so many of us! We wear shorts, loose linen dresses, t-shirts with faded logos and lyrics –

heaven is a place on earth. *

Tiny children wobble in play parks; fountains giggle over their pure skin. Young men on paddleboards travel the loop of the river that unwinds round the city, like floating Adonises, stroking and breaking the water's skein, calling to each other, splashing, yelling.

We stop on the library steps, gulp from plastic bottles, watch the city that has turned itself inside out – so many of us!

Silence has made us paler. We swear we've never seen that patch of skin before. Our thighs are plump like dough; they've been so good for sleeping on. They brush together, whisper when we walk –

this far, we've come.

* A Belinda Carlisle song.

Rise

For months, we've had a bellyful of stones.

In the city's heart, there is a glorious high-rise. Inside, a glittering hallway with an elevator serving G to 55. See your masks in its mirrored sides. The ride, the floor within us

falling.

Step out of confinement, the streets un-scroll below us. Remember what air feels like? Lift your hands, let the wind take and fill you. Get on your knees, skin to raw surface, bend your head and kiss concrete, make murmurs, that sound something like –

God, help us.

Holiday Inn, Babylon Central

The Corporate Entertainment Suite has been converted to a gym. At intervals, Hope comes in. She wears a badge – 'Pure Gym' – and checks things over, and over again: blue paper towels, pink spray bottles for wipe-downs, empty the bin.

Behind the metal grille, the bar still glows, polished walnut wood and glass. Empty upturned glasses, Corona buckets and Pepsi taps, dry as bones.

Dumbbells and kettlebells are arranged, light to heavy, heavy to light, on the carpet. The treadmills squat like robots with empty arms. They blink in silence, watch. There's a man's back in a mirror. He works a cross-trainer, climbing a mountain of air.

Over time, Hope starts to notice things: unspent crystals in salt cellars; strange circles on the murky carpet; red digit eyes of the machines. She gnaws at the toughened bit of skin on her right index finger; it tastes like swimming pools. She is sure that she can see particles hanging in the artificially chilled air, pink and static.

Early in the mornings, Hope rows this air, cycles it, hammers it onto a moving surface. Breathing is inevitable. Sweat trickles, settles in the crow's feet round her eyes, slides towards the cusp of her upper lip, collects under both breasts, a darkness.

The cabbie (1)

He works nights, passing blue lights. Silence. Blue lights. But the streets are magic after dark.

He doesn't need Satnav or stars. He knows Babylon's backstreets like his daughters and sons, like their voices in the morning, their feet on the carpeted stairs.

While she cooks, nags, worries, gets them to bed, pours a drink, watches the news, he criss-crosses the city, office blocks to station forecourt to banks to city outskirts. Fare after fare, the night goes. He doesn't miss conversation much. He's learned to read his fares behind the glass like texts – it's all in the eyes, above the mask. He observes the way they watch empty pavements, traffic lights, like they're adverts.

He curses the gulls –

fucking birds.

He takes this city, while it's sleeping, while no one else is looking, slipping lane to lane like he's a king, and in between, he sings, picturing her warm and safe in his bed, breathing.

He doesn't know when it will end. He thanks God he is working.

The Argentine tango teacher (1)

She stands
in the centre of the polished floor,
a version of herself
in the mirrored wall.
She's turned the speakers up full;
violin notes drag and curve over strummed guitar.
The bow clings to the strings,
obsesses,
penetrates her chest.
The sound swells up and down the empty dancehall,
leaches through open doors and out
into the industrial estate, out
into the cul-de-sacs, out
into the backyards beyond.

It's three in the afternoon.
The air sits like a crust
over Babylon.

A hand is held out
from an open window.
Its fingers know a cigarette;
every few beats,
they flick ash into heavy sunlight.

The violin comes
and goes,
torpid birdsong.
Somebody coughs.
The streets and alleys sweat it out.

She clicks her heels,
watches herself
begin to dance.

A busker plays Amy

with lyrics from Amy Winehouse's song 'Love is a losing game'

He stands at the corner of Commercial Centre, a burgundy tunic, gold
kufi cap. His duffle bag is gaping on the cobbles by his feet, showing
its coins like few teeth. He holds the sax close, sways, breathes,
blows, like loving her and losing her at the same time

Five-storey fire

People stop to watch his mouth and they are baptised in sound. A lad
passing on the other side of the street twists away to gob

Mocked by the gods

A mother hands her boy some loose change; he steps forward, held in
the purple sound, lets the coins fall

Five-storey fire

now airborne.

The ones who turned 18

Babylon's streets turn out the young like sequins under stars.
Clicking heels, pre-party laughs, goofy shouts, glossy selfies, sweaty
hands. Tonight, they remember what they forgot.

Close in on midnight. Outside Skn, they queue around the block; faces
glow in the light of phones. 11.59: a pair of boys in matching orange
catsuits, flashing red horns, start the shout –

5, 4, 3, 2...

hoots go up, doors are flung open, check-in starts. All borders
breached, dissolved in the bottom of the glass. Here, there's no apart.
It wasn't their fault. They will shed skin tonight.

Act Two

Mantra

I'll run if you run. Run after me. Run from the city. Run to the
junction, the corner, the crest of the hill. Maybe, to the ocean. Run to
find out. To see what we know. Run to find out what we have
forgotten. Run to burn time. Run to unbind. Run to feel pressure. Run
to hurl fire. Run to protect and run to remember.

The Argentine tango teacher (2)

She watches herself
begin to dance –
chin high, hands scrunch the hips
of her black dress;
her legs step, slide.
Tequila burns inside her
as she tries to remember
what it felt like –
step, slide –
to cling to his neck,
his arm hooked round the small of her back;
the violin climbs higher –
hot breath under her ear,
his hand gripping her raised thigh –
step, slide.

Her torso's tensioned, springs;
the violin bemoans the loss of him.
She ball-swivels, kicks, hooks, twists,
holds,
suspends breath,
remembers the fire she'd been
between his legs,
no space,
twisted together, ropes of satin.

The notes rise to the top,
drop,
slow.

Her body poured out,
black song in the mirror.

Swing low, sweet chariot

Pressure is high, but then, this is summer. The Avenue limes rustle like paper. Something is coming. At noon, a call to prayer. This day could spark, catch, go up in flames.

The city is filling. Tonight, for the first time in oh so many years, the Stadium will see 80 thousand packed in.

Car horns puncture the ring road. Barbecue smoke spreads like smutty laughter from yard to yard. Kids' hype ricochets off walls, bundles between parked cars, flips skateboards, floods the backs of houses, alleyways. Deliveroos prepare to criss-cross the residential streets, their bikes on standby. The people are hungry.

Sports pub screens play the pre-pre-match commentary. The delicious *Will they, Won't they*. Shirts on backs are already damp with sweat, booze, hysteria. Thousands on sofas, bar stools, benches, dying for any seat in the house, for a taste of the beautiful combat.

Rising from inside the arena, 80 thousand prayers to the gods. 80 thousand crying for sweet, sweet victory with hot, unmasked breath.

31 degrees

and the trees know it, heat tempering their scales, making limb bones pliant, warming rings within rings. They stretch up, needles taut, to gather the gold, backs sticky with sap.

Sun on freckles, sun on the girl, she rolls up her blanket. 31 degrees. Saunters zig-zag into woods. Under the trees all things are closer and sweeter. A blackbird hops then sings, makes air curl into her, stunning.

Will you stay?

the trees are asking. In the soil they cradle her, reach out and touch, roots tumid but good. They have no word for ██████ though they've known it before. They lift arched roots, gateways to other times, other places. The girl spins on the spot, head loose and dizzied by burgeoning elderflower, luminescent lime-leafed ceilings, cedar, cedar. She spins and forgets.

Olympic Aquatics Centre

On the screen, we watch them stride out under artificial lights. No crowds, just vacant plastic seats and cameras. Their blank skin shines, like seals. Their heads and shoulders bear solemnity, silence. They do not think of us.

The camera drones seek them out. Pan: swivel: focus: close-up:

good.

The summer night presses its heat into the bricks and glass inside us. The electric fan makes another pass. It's almost midnight. Here, on our sofas, in the glow of TV screens, we fantasise – contoured chest, sinewed thighs. We breathe and whisper to ourselves –

They are us; they are ours.

Countdown. Watch them dive:
twin

thunder.

Later, we dream of an infinite dome kissing water. We stand on tiptoe
then we
fall

fall

all

Sundays

Go past the Doner Kebab, Bookies, Tanning Booth, Boundary Bar &
Grill, Minimarket, Blue Mango. Go down towards the red brick
Temple, down towards the twin high-rises. Between them, a single-
storey building with a shiny banner, the sound of wooden upright
piano, voices, treading old hymns –

His love endures forever.

The chorus shifts, escapes, drifts out the open door to the high-rises,
to a balcony where a man leans against the railings, his mouth a shut
line. He closes his eyes, lets the railings take the weight of his
shoulders. They are as heavy as wings. The notes rise higher, catch in
wet washing strung between chairs –

His love

in cracked empty flowerpots, in strings of fairy lights, the shape of
stars.

Night Security Guard, Orion, Floor 55, Commercial Centre

That feeling of water. Like earlier. Standing naked, looking up,
waiting for the last slow drop from the shower head.

He looks out, into the black glass panorama below, pricked with
artificial lights. He can't see it but he knows the river encircles the
city in the dark. He knows water cannot protect us. He sees a vixen
streak between streetlamps, rusty scrap of bones and fur and hunger.
He thinks he sees a pair of rats trickle down a fence. He hears the
gulls agitating. Like him, they never sleep.

During the curfew spell, it was stranger than now. He'd go all night
and barely see a soul inside or out, just flashing blues and helicopters,
slicing the silence. But tonight, if he sits close to the glass and stares
beyond his own face, he can make out frantic bikes that speed
through pedestrian zones in the dark, shuttling hot food in padded
bags to couples flaked out in front of TVs. He knows that outside, as
the gull flies, miles and miles, there is sea...queues of HGVs, testing
stations, checkpoints. He has forgotten what sea smells like.

Blue Mango, Church Quarter

Let's show face. Let's queue down the street, round the corner,
brimming, slippery and shining like a net of sardines. Let's surge like
children, fill this club like a deep breath

in

to bursting. Let's cramp the bar, hands calling, pull each other
through, wading, all the time chanting lost nicknames, old poisons.
We're wide open.

Now elevate hands, 2-for-1s, lit phones. Brush arms and arms and
legs, breathe no air except everybody's

exhale.

Spill salt, sugar, blood from our heels. The bass shakes the laughter
from our throats and eyes. Read lips, touch palms and move to the
floor, know again what bodies are for. Vibrate, translate, fix on beats
that take our heads off, screw them on.

Babylon! Open your dangerous mouth, now
sing!

Act Three

Ping

When we get notified, we will slow-blink our eyes, close the door, with only us inside. We will then observe all guidelines.

We are advised to inform our employer: *the lights in my house are out.* We are advised to throw open the window, breathe in light. We are advised to message all our friends. We are ill-advised to make love or spit at our wife. We are advised that this should not be possible, anyway. (See above.) We are advised to update our status, if we know what our status is. We are advised to use water, in any of its forms, in any way that we can. Remember that there is always rain, an open window. We are advised that, after three days, the colour of light will change. We are advised to update our followers on this. We are advised that blackbirds grow brash outside. We are advised to use Google Translate, to help understand. When the house is silent, we are advised to enter the kitchen, take out a tin of beans, consume them. Watch the washing machine. Cheer it, when it spins. We are advised to get back, quickly. We are advised to tell our daughter, *No*, through the crack. We are advised to message the friends that replied. We are advised that, after five days, our skin will look strange. We are strongly advised not to look. We are advised that the blackbirds become gulls become brutalisers. We are advised to update our followers on this. We are advised to close our eyes. We are advised to fling our phones.

Remember that open window?

The blind man of Babylon

When he sits on the stone steps of the Civic Hall, facing the street,
eating his sandwich, he knows the mewing of the gulls, knows they're
perched like statues beside pilasters behind him, knows their backs
are mottled brown; they are young, they are waiting.

When he returns to his desk in the office building, behind the screens,
he knows each footfall, who is passing. He knows it's not a desk
phone ringing; it's a bush somewhere, burning.

At home, he knows the night is coming. He slips the record from its
sleeve, the scent of old paper and whisky, places it on the turntable,
expertly, to know how and why she is, for what is dancing, if it isn't
taking her in your arms and knowing?

Lying on the sofa, all things are ending when he feels the needle
shush the last ripple on the vinyl

and shush

and shush

    and shush.

She hides (1)

On a campus. In a concrete block. On a given level. Accessed only by stairwell. Door after door after door. Fire doors, of course, *health and safety*.

Her small square window looks out on a red brick wall. She leaves the bed and desk and this window, sometimes. She enters the kitchen area, sometimes. Caution. This is *communal*.

She has returned with a plate of pasta, a glass of water. She pokes her key in the lock, turns. The door self-closes behind her. Fire doors, remember?

She folds herself onto the bed, props her plate on her knees, looks towards the square window, that lets in not a lot of light.

A gull crosses.

Every few minutes, a gull crosses.

She thinks they are arrows; they fly with such purpose.

The cabbie (2)

A wet night. His shortcut. A spray of gulls overhead, over warehouse rooves. Their rain-softened bodies, open wings, catch the bright spill from floodlights and he sees they are white doves, sent out after the flood.

She hides (2)

In her block, behind her door, on the floor, there are stacks of books, up and up and up. Her ziggurats, made of words.

At night, she lies on her back in bed, listens to laughter that cracks in the kitchen, a clatter of pan lids, doors flying open, self-slamming. There's a slot of light, under the door, which will be replaced by heavy daylight, come morning.

Sometimes, she misses Babylon, but it's alright. She has her city of words.

In the dark, the fine hair on her body turns to hollow shafts, downy whiteness. Her heart beats pale and fast. She can harness air, whip it with feathered arms, force it back. She surges, circles round and round her paper towers.

Here, there are no masks. She eyes the highest point, lowers with skill, plants her gaudy feet, sheathes her wings. She opens her mouth – clean and precise as porcelain. Like a siren, her cries pour out.

The man and his dog

You pass a man in the park. He throws a word of greeting at your feet, at a distance, as you cross paths. He's followed by a small pilgrim – white dog, that lingers at your ankles. Your heart squeezes.

She won't hurt ya none.

You bend down, to touch her. You want her to stay, at your feet, talk to you, with her gleaming eyes, but she turns towards the voice. You want him to stop walking away. You want him to tell you if there is harm. You want him to tell you the truth of everything.

She hides (3)

She wakes to the nudge of morning, feels the bedclothes trap her skin, remembers all the bones of her real feet and hands.

Today, she will try again to go outside.

Kings

In the open-air amphitheatre that is University Square, the fountain is back on. Water droplets tickle, darken, wake up the stone. A pigeon edges along, wiry pink feet tap-tap, orange eye down, looking for flecks of crumb. Water droplets fall, transform his ordinary neck to emeralds and amethysts in the sunlight.

Soon, this will be real theatre again, thrumming with the rainbow of beautiful people criss-crossing, milling, lingering to catch each other for a moment, to squeal in delight –

I haven't seen you in soooooo long!

They've folded back the doors of the SU building, pinned them open onto the terrace above. Inside, a masked boy is playing 'We Three Kings' on a hollow piano. He's stop-starting, playing the same phrases over and over again* –

Born a King

Gold I bring

The sky promises late summer rain. The boy plays. The pigeon swivels its head, orange eye to the sky, twitches a wing –

field and fountain, moor and mountain

* Lyrics from the hymn 'We Three Kings Of Orient Are'

Epilogue

Beyond the city

we hear rumours like sonar echoes in seas. Nations grow in shadows. Reportedly, a destroyer in someone else's territory. Raw data, points on a graph and carefully worded responses –

We do not Authorise. Borders are Closed. According to our Sources.

A family is halted by border patrol, required to show the colour of their passports.

We listen for other tides, other music, for mothers and sons who dance.

Prayer

After 'Author's prayer' by Ilya Kaminsky

If I speak for the dead, I must first bleach my heart feather-white –
I am not holy enough.

If I speak for the dead, heart wired to my mouth, my mouth will make
the shape of them; they emerge, moth-like.

When I speak for the dead, I pour out salt.

When I speak for the dead, I call on a God whose name is white heat.

If I speak for the dead, I know it may not bring them back.

The secret history of anger (2)

After 'In Praise of Laughter' by Ilya Kaminsky

Anger is taken from the fire. It cools.

The woman has kept silence long enough.

Dawn arrives. God anoints her,

like the dew.

ELAINE BAKER is a poet, teacher and mentor, now living in Breckland, Norfolk. She loves leading writing workshops for the next generation and has been working with neurodivergent young writers on the Beyond the Spectrum Project (pioneered by Writing East Midlands) for the past 3 years. Elaine has an MA in Writing Poetry from The Poetry School/Newcastle University, and her experience of relocating to the city of Norwich in 2020 became the catalyst that led to the writing of this book. *Dancing in Babylon* is her third poetry chapbook, following *five-point-palm* (Red Ceilings Press, 2021) and *Winter with Eva* (V Press, 2020). A full list of her published work can be found on her website: www.elaine-baker.com.